MEOW

by Roger Hargreaves

HODDER AND STOUGHTON
LONDON SYDNEY AUCKLAND TORONTO

Meow was a sort of cat.
A Timbuctoo cat.
He lived in Marmalade Cottage.
In Timbuctoo.

He woke up one morning.
"What a nice day," he cried, leaping out of bed.
"How shall I spend it?"

"I know," he thought. "I'll go fishing !"
Meow had never been fishing before, and because he didn't know anything about it he went out and bought himself a book.
All about it.
And off he set down to the river.
He sat himself down under a tree and opened the book.
"Fishing," said the book, "is easy !"
"Good," said Meow.
"First," said the book, "find a river."
Meow looked up.
"One river," he said.

"Next," said the book, "find a piece of string!"
Meow put the book down, ran home to Marmalade Cottage, and came back with a piece of string.
"Well done," said the book.

"Next," said the book, "find a rod, and tie the string to it."
Meow looked up.
"Find a road ?" he said.
"Not a road," went on the book. "A rod ! And the best rod," it said, "is a branch from a tree."
So Meow went off, and found a branch, and tied the piece of string to it.

"Next," said the book, "find a pin."
So, Meow put the book down again,
and again ran home to Marmalade Cottage,
and came back with a pin.

"Tie the pin onto the end of the string," said the book.
So Meow did.
"Next," went on the book, "fix some bait to the pin."
"Bait ?" said Meow. "What's bait ?"
"Bait," went on the book, "is something fish like to eat."

Meow thought.
"I wonder what fish like to eat ?"
he thought.
The tree he was sitting under was an apple tree ! !
"That should do," he thought, and fixed an apple to the pin.
"Now," said the book, "you are ready to start fishing."
"Good," said Meow.

"Cast the line into the river,"
went on the book.
"Cast?" said Meow. "What's cast?"
"Cast," said the book, "means throw!"

Meow smiled.
And threw his fishing line into the river.

Not just the line.
The rod.
The bait.
Everything !
Silly cat !

"And now," continued the book, "sit there until you catch something."
Meow sat there all morning.
And all afternoon.

And sat there all night.
"Fishing's not what I would call a
lot of fun," he thought.

In the morning a fish poked his head out of the water.
"What are you doing ?" asked the fish.
"I'm trying," explained Meow, "to catch you."

The fish chuckled.
"There's only one thing you're going to catch if you sit around on river banks all night," he said.

"What's that ?" asked Meow.
"The only thing you're going to catch," repeated the fish, "is a cold !"
"Atishoo !" sneezed Meow.
"Told you so," said the fish.